FIGHTING FORCES
ON LAND

M109 PALADIN

DAVID BAKER

Rourke
Publishing LLC
Vero Beach, Florida 32964

www.rourkepublishing.com

PHOTO CREDITS: All photos courtesy United States Department of Defense, United States Department of the Army, BAe Systems

Title page: *The M109 has been sold to several countries including Germany, Italy, Israel, Taiwan, and Egypt.*

Editor: Robert Stengard-Olliges

Library of Congress Cataloging-in-Publication Data

Baker, David, 1944-
 M109 Paladin / David Baker.
    p. cm. -- (Fighting forces on land)
 Includes index.
 "Further Reading/Websites"--p.32.
 ISBN 1-60044-245-5
 1. M109 Paladin (Howitzer)--Juvenile literature. I. Title. II. Series.
 UF652.B35 2007
 623.4'2--dc22
                                2006010783

Printed in the USA

CG/CG

Rourke Publishing

www.rourkepublishing.com – sales@rourkepublishing.com
Post Office Box 3328, Vero Beach, FL 32964

TABLE OF CONTENTS

CHAPTER ONE

THE SELF PROPELLED GUN

From the outset, artillery has had to be mobile so that big guns could be brought to appropriate positions within range of enemy targets but defended from opposing fire. Several hundred years ago, men dragged big guns to the field of action. Women operated and fired the guns while the men performed heavy labor. As guns got bigger horses pulled them to the front line.

▲

The M109 has been popular with foreign armies including Israel seen here operating one of their howitzers bought from the US.

▲

The development of large towed siege howitzers reached its peak during World War I (1914-1918) as represented by this 105 mm French artillery piece.

▲

By World War II (1939-1945) guns were lighter and more mobile. This British 25 lb gun achieved fame during the desert wars in North Africa during 1941-1943.

By the time of the American Civil War (1861-1865), several thousand horses were used for this purpose by Union and Confederate forces. When **motorized** transport appeared during World War I (1914-1918) the guns could be hauled around by special vehicles operating like tractors. There was, however, a special kind of gun that needed an integral form of motive power to achieve not just **portability** but mobility, too.

Assault guns and assault howitzers evolved from field artillery to support infantry by bombarding enemy positions and weakening the **opposition**. Towed artillery is slow because it has to be set up before it can fire whereas self-propelled artillery (howitzers) can respond faster, advance or withdraw at will, and drive quickly to another sector ready for immediate action.

▲

A 105 mm US Army howitzer bombards the outskirts of Baghdad during the overthrow of Iraq's ruler Saddam Hussein.

This light artillery 105 mm M119 howitzer can be towed
by a Humvee or dropped by air. Weighing two tons, it has
a range of almost nine miles.

CHAPTER TWO

GOING TO WAR IN A CADILLAC

Self-propelled artillery proved itself during World War II (1939-1945) and became an integral part of modern assault tactics during the Korean Conflict (1950-1953). When US forces became involved in South Vietnam against communist guerrillas during the mid and late 1960s, medium self-propelled guns played their part in breaking resistance. However, the greatest use of the self propelled howitzer was seen to devastating effect in the big battles of the Middle East in wars between Israel and the Arab states and between Iraq and Iran in the 1980s.

Self-propelled howitzers carry their own ammunition, provide protection for the gun crew, and are mobile without additional support. This 155 mm M109 bombards positions in the former Yugoslavia that collapsed into civil war during the 1990s.

With its rear door open for additional ventilation a US Army M109 fires on the outskirts of Baghdad. Note the 0.5 caliber M2 machine gun on a traversing mount.

In 1952, during the Korean Conflict, the US Army stated an urgent need for a modern self-propelled howitzer and designed a 156 mm **caliber** gun. A few years later in 1956, NATO (North Atlantic Treaty Organization) standardized the caliber for big guns at 155 mm. The T196, precursor to the M109, was selected for detailed design with a gun of this caliber.

▲

Buttoned down for maximum protection, this M109 firing a 98 lb shell demonstrates the self-contained concept of the self-propelled howitzer.

In 1959, the Army stipulated a **diesel** rather than a gasoline engine. In October 1961, the Army contracted Cadillac Motor Car Division to develop the howitzer chassis and track arrangement at the Cleveland Army Tank Plant. The first production vehicles rolled out in 1962 and in late 1963, the Chrysler Corporation received a contract to put the vehicle into large-scale production.

With two sprocket wheels and seven road wheels, each side of the M109 has a simple yet rugged track and drive system with good maneuverability.

CHAPTER THREE

NEW WEAPONS FOR NEW YEARS

The M109 went through a range of versions from the outset. The first model was the M109 SPH with a very short barrel firing shells a maximum range of nine miles and a large fume extractor, replaced by the M109A1 SPH with a longer barrel with a firing range of more than 11 miles. When the M109A2 appeared it had many improvements and a broad range of new operational capabilities including increased stowage for more ammunition, new targeting and alignment devices, and a new and more efficient gun mount.

◀ *The breach mechanism of the M109 operated by a gunner gets very hot during rapid sequential firing and limits the number of rounds per minute fired at enemy positions.*

▲

Operating behind the lines, the M109 has more internal volume than the M1A1 Abrams main battle tank because it does not have to deflect incoming shells or have reduced frontal area for hiding from attack.

▲

The advantages of the towed M119 also limit its use. Although it is light and easy to move, it requires a tow vehicle, a supply truck to carry ammunition, and has a relatively short range.

Uploading target alignment and firing commands prior to firing a round from the 155 mm gun.

▲
A typical towed-gun crew; notice the ranging plotter working with a laptop at extreme left.

The A3 was virtually identical to the A2, however the A4 introduced fully modernized crew safety and operating function for any anticipated form of **nuclear**, chemical, or **biological** warfare. This included an air filtration system to prevent the crew from breathing in poisonous or **toxic** fumes. With a new gun and further refinements, the A5 was the last of the original line of developments before the introduction of a considerably modified version, the A6 Paladin, in several respects a completely new vehicle and fire control system.

The M109A6 Paladin can fire up to four rounds per minute for three minutes or maintain a sustained rate of one round per minute depending on sensors that warn of excess heat in the gun.

FIREPOWER

The M109A6, named Paladin, is the most technologically advanced 155 mm howitzer available anywhere in the world. It is equipped with special computers that can work out precisely where it is on the ground and, with intelligence information on the exact position of the target; it can compute firing angles and **azimuth** (the amount of degrees the turret and barrel is slewed to left or right) for precise firing data.

▲

Bombarding Fallujah, Iraq, during Operation Iraqi Freedom in 2003.

▲

The advantages of the self-propelled howitzer have encouraged development of similar types by many armies around the world. Here, Singapore's 155 mm Primus shows off its rugged design.

Previously, wires would have to be laid between the six tracked M109 vehicles in a **battery** and a fire control center set up nearby. **Surveyors** would have to calculate the relative position of the battery to the known location of the target, an operation that would take about 20 minutes to complete before the guns were ready to fire. With the A6 Paladin that job is done automatically, without wires, the first round fired within 45 seconds of coming to a halt. Moreover, where before it took another 20 minutes to roll up all the wires and move out it now takes less than a minute.

A modern battery of six guns firing 100 lb shells at four rounds per minute will throw more than 1 ton of **ordnance** each minute for up to four minutes, all of which is delivered with great **accuracy** and effectiveness. That gets the attention of the enemy and any howitzer crew that stays around too long can expect an incoming artillery barrage. This is why it is as important to leave as quickly as you arrived. As an added advantage, the Paladin can fire on the move, getting target and position data from **satellites**.

▲

Artillerymen set up a towed howitzer with a vulnerable supply truck loaded with ammunition.

CHAPTER FIVE

BUILDING ON THE BASIC

Although the M109A6 Paladin has been around for a few years, it too is getting upgrades and improvements to maintain its edge over the enemy, who will always seek ways to take out the artillery before it can do its job. With a top speed of 35 mph and a range of almost 190 miles, the 62 ton tracked howitzer is a **formidable** assault weapon and the four-man crew of the A6 version can throw powerful 155 mm shells every 25 seconds to a maximum range of more than 20 miles. Literally a "shoot-and-scoot" assault gun, the A6 Paladin bridges the gap between the basic M109 and its successor yet to come, secured to serve the Army for many more years of service.

Flexible and adaptable, the M109 is in service with US forces around the globe. This example of all weather capability captures a moment in the former Yugoslavia in the Balkans, southeastern Europe.

Glossary

accuracy (AK yuh ruh cee) – without mistakes or error

azimuth (AZ meth) – the horizontal component of a compass direction, used to determine direction to aim guns

battery (BAT uh ree) – a group of machines or heavy guns that are all used together

biological (bye ol LOJ ikal) – organisms or toxins found in nature

caliber (CAL uh ber) – the diameter of the barrel of a gun

diesel (DEE zuhl) – a fuel used in diesel engines that is heavier than gasoline

formidable (FOR muh duh buhl) – having qualities that discourage approach or attack

motorized (MOH tur izeed) – equipped with a motor or engine

nuclear (NOO klee ur) – to do with energy caused by splitting atoms, a weapon that used the power from splitting atoms

opposition (op uh ZISH uhn) – hostile action, a group of people opposed to something

ordnance (ORD nents) – military supplies including weapons, ammunition, combat vehicles, and equipment

portability (POR tuh buhl uh tee) – able to be easily moved to a new location

satellite (SAT uh lite) – a spacecraft in orbit around the earth often used in communication networks

surveyor (sur VAY or) – a person who measures an area to make a map or a plan

toxic (TOK sik) – poisonous

INDEX

FURTHER READING

Green, Michael and Gladys. *Self-Propelled Howitzers: The M109A6 Paladins*. Edge Books, 2004

Matsumura, John. *Assessment of Crusader: The Army's Next Self Propelled Howitzer and Resupply Vehicle*. Rand Corporation, 1998

WEBSITES TO VISIT

http://www.wikipedia.org/wiki/M1

http://www.army-technology.com/projects/abrams

ABOUT THE AUTHOR

David Baker is a specialist in defense and space programs, author of more than 60 books and consultant to many government and industry organizations. David is also a lecturer and policy analyst and regularly visits many countries around the world in the pursuit of his work.

ML .

1/07